Lerner **SPORTS**™

SPORTS ALL-ST★RS

DREW BREES

Jon M. Fishman

Lerner Publications ● Minneapolis

Lerner Publications Company
An imprint of Lerner Publishing Group, Inc.
241 First Avenue North
Minneapolis, MN 55401 USA

For reading levels and more information, look up this title at www.lernerbooks.com.

Main body text set in Albany Std.Typeface provided by Agfa.

Library of Congress Cataloging-in-Publication Data

Names: Fishman, Jon M., author.
Title: Drew Brees / Jon M. Fishman.
Description: Minneapolis : Lerner Publications, [2020] | Series: Sports all-stars | Includes bibliographical references and index.
Identifiers: LCCN 2019016943 (print) | LCCN 2019019576 (ebook) | ISBN 9781541583559 (eb pdf) | ISBN 9781541577275 (lb : alk. paper) | ISBN 9781541589537 (pb : alk. paper)
Subjects: LCSH: Brees, Drew, 1979– —Juvenile literature. | Football players—United States—Biography—Juvenile literature. | Quarterbacks (Football)—United States—Biography—Juvenile literature.
Classification: LCC GV939.B695 (ebook) | LCC GV939.B695 F57 2020 (print) | DDC 796.332092 [B]—dc23

LC record available at https://lccn.loc.gov/2019016943

Manufactured in the United States of America
1-46749-47740-9/16/2019

CONTENTS

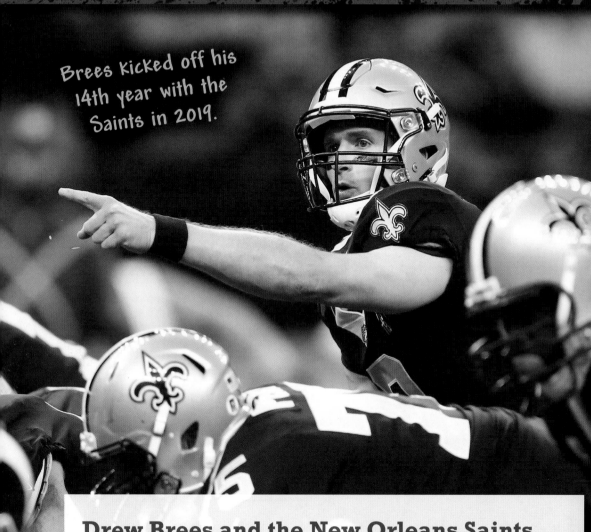

Brees kicked off his 14th year with the Saints in 2019.

Drew Brees and the New Orleans Saints were getting crushed. It was January 13, 2019, at the National Football League (NFL) playoffs, and the Philadelphia Eagles led 14-0 in the first quarter.

- **Date of Birth:** January 15, 1979

- **Position:** quarterback

- **League:** NFL

- **Professional Highlights:** came back from a severe shoulder injury; won the Super Bowl with the Saints in 2010; set the NFL's all-time passing yards record in 2018

- **Personal Highlights:** played sports with his younger brother, Reid; donated more than $33 million to charity through his foundation; has four children

Brees (right) reacts to a missed catch during the 2019 playoffs.

The losing team would be out of the playoffs, their season finished.

The Eagles were the defending Super Bowl champions. They had one of the league's toughest defenses. If the Saints were going to win, they needed to start their comeback. But it was fourth down with one yard to go. The Saints got ready to **punt**.

New Orleans coaches called a trick play. The team lined up in a punt **formation**. But the team **snapped** the ball to running back Taysom Hill instead of the kicker. Hill ran for a four-yard gain and a first down. The fake punt worked!

Suddenly the Saints' comeback was underway. Brees passed to wide receiver Michael Thomas for a 42-yard gain. A few plays later, Brees threw a short touchdown pass to Keith Kirkwood. That made the score 14–7.

By the third quarter, the Saints were still behind 14–10. Then Brees led his team on one of the most epic scoring drives of the season. From the eight-yard line, the Saints moved the ball 92 yards down the field. The 18-play drive lasted 11 minutes and 29 seconds and took up most of the third quarter. It ended when Brees passed to Thomas for a touchdown.

The score gave New Orleans a 17–14 lead. They added three points in the fourth quarter and won the game 20–14. The Saints stayed confident with Brees leading the way, even when they were losing by two touchdowns. "We were real calm and **poised** and we knew we were going to get things done," Brees said.

Brees has led the Saints to comeback wins many times. He has 34 fourth-quarter comebacks in his career. That ties him with Johnny Unitas for third most fourth-quarter comebacks ever.

TALL ENOUGH

The Purdue Boilermakers reached both a Big Ten Championship and a Rose Bowl with Brees as their quarterback.

Drew Brees was born on January 15, 1979, in Austin, Texas. When he was seven years old, his parents divorced. Drew and his younger brother, Reid, spent time living with both of their parents.

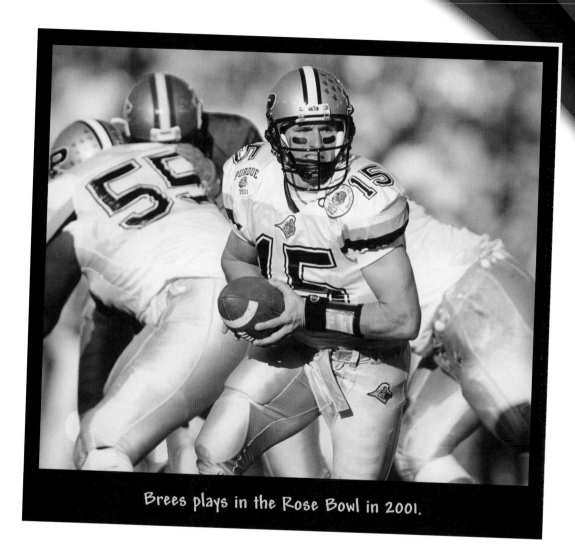

Brees plays in the Rose Bowl in 2001.

Moving back and forth between homes was hard on the boys. They relied on each other for support. One of their favorite things to do was compete in sports. They golfed, played Ping-Pong, and threw horseshoes. They even had seed-spitting contests.

At Westlake High School in Austin, Drew played basketball, baseball, and football. He was an excellent quarterback and led his team to an unbeaten season his senior year. He wanted to play college football, but most teams weren't interested. He had injured his knee as a junior in 1996. But the main reason many college teams ignored him was his height.

Drew stood 6 feet (1.8 m) tall. Most college quarterbacks are taller. To be a good quarterback, a player must be able to see all around the field. Some coaches worried Drew wouldn't be able to see over taller college players.

Brees's record of 90 touchdown passes held for almost 15 years after he left Purdue.

But coaches at Purdue University in West Lafayette, Indiana, believed in Drew. They offered him a **scholarship** to join the school's football team. He accepted and moved to Indiana.

Brees played his first games for Purdue in 1997. In 1998, he became the team's starting quarterback and a star of the Big Ten **Conference**. That season he threw an amazing 39 touchdowns and helped Purdue reach a record of 9–4.

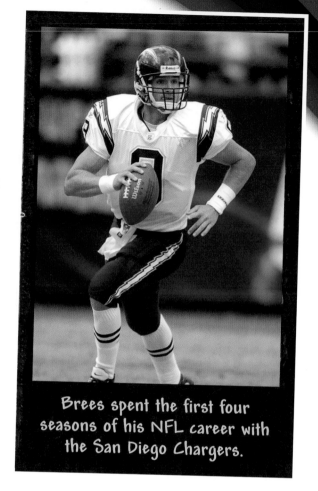

Brees spent the first four seasons of his NFL career with the San Diego Chargers.

By the time Brees left Purdue in 2000, he held the all-time conference record with 90 touchdown passes. He still holds the Big Ten record for career passing yards with 11,792. Brees had proved he could succeed at college football. But he still had to convince **scouts** he could play in the NFL.

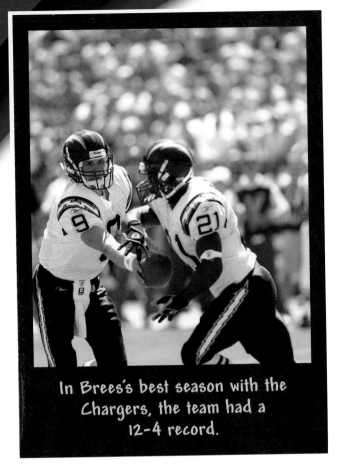

In Brees's best season with the Chargers, the team had a 12-4 record.

Brees entered the 2001 NFL **draft**. The San Diego Chargers selected him with the first pick in the second round. He became San Diego's starting quarterback in 2002. But he didn't have much success at first. In 2003, he threw more **interceptions** than touchdowns.

Brees hurt his throwing shoulder during the 2005 season. To avoid paying an injured quarterback millions of dollars, the Chargers let him go to another team. He joined the New Orleans Saints. The Saints had faith in Brees, and that meant a lot to him. "They believe I can come back from this shoulder injury and lead them to a championship," he said.

Brees was injured where his shoulder joint, shown in this X-ray, rotated. The injury meant he couldn't throw.

The Saints were taking a chance on Brees. His shoulder injury was severe. His doctor, James Andrews, wasn't sure Brees would ever play in the NFL again.

Doctors told Brees he wouldn't play for two years after his injury. But by the end of 2006, he was practicing with the Saints.

Brees had surgery to repair the injury in January 2006. To get back on the field as quickly as possible, Brees started **rehab** right after surgery. He spent up to eight hours a day working to heal his shoulder. A trainer taught him exercises to build his muscles back up. Brees also worked to keep the rest of his body fit.

He began throwing footballs again about four weeks after surgery. He also restarted his work with trainer Todd Durkin. Brees and Durkin had worked together since 2003.

Unlike many NFL players, Brees doesn't lift heavy weights. He focuses on keeping his muscles healthy and **agile**. He wants training to be as intense as NFL games. Durkin directs him in fast-paced workouts. They move quickly from one exercise to the next.

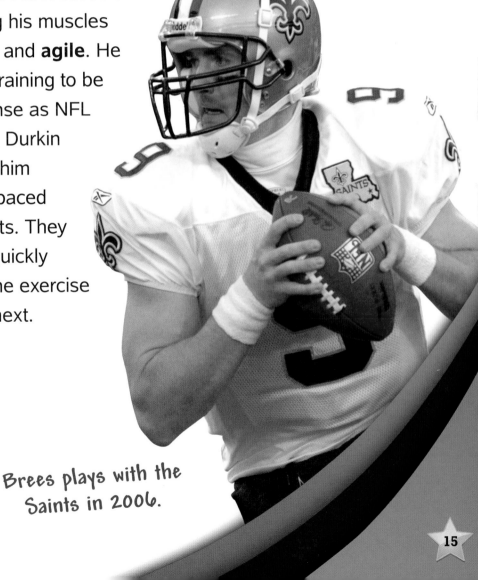

Brees plays with the Saints in 2006.

On a normal workout day, Brees starts with stretches and movements to loosen his joints and muscles. He pays special attention to his right shoulder to help prevent another injury. He might use elastic bands in some of the exercises. Then he grabs heavy ropes and shakes them to strengthen his shoulders. Brees and Durkin also use high-tech gear such as elastic harnesses. Brees does push-ups and other moves while a harness holds his feet in the air.

Brees makes sure to stretch and warm up before games.

During the season, Brees gets up at about five every morning. During the off-season, he gets up even earlier. That way he can have time to himself before his four children wake up.

Brees has said his shoulder injury turned into a good thing. He learned how to make his body stronger than before.

By the start of the 2006 season, Brees was ready to play again. Andrews said it was "the most remarkable comeback that I've ever treated." After a lot of hard work, Brees's shoulder was stronger than ever. He was ready to make the New Orleans Saints champions.

PAYBACK

Brees plays in the Superdome on September 25, 2006, the day the Superdome reopened after Hurricane Katrina.

Hurricane Katrina damaged the roof of the Superdome, causing parts of the stadium to flood.

Brees was healing when he joined the Saints. So was New Orleans. In August 2005, Hurricane Katrina destroyed much of the city. The storm damaged the Superdome, the Saints' home stadium. It stayed closed for a year.

On September 25, 2006, the Superdome finally reopened. In his first home game with his new team, Brees led the Saints to victory over the Atlanta Falcons 23–3. The win and the reopening of the Superdome made many in New Orleans proud. "That was just a symbol that this city was going to come back, not only the way it was before, but better than it was before," Brees said.

Brees and teammate Jammal Brown celebrate their first victory in the new Superdome.

Man of the Year

Brees made a special connection with the people of New Orleans. As he healed from shoulder surgery, he helped the city heal from Hurricane Katrina. "I needed somebody to believe in me just as much as New Orleans needed someone to believe in them," he said.

Brees used his money and superstar status to aid the city. He helped rebuild football fields and playgrounds for kids and took part in many other projects. In 2006, the NFL honored him. Brees and former teammate LaDainian Tomlinson won the Walter Payton Man of the Year award. The NFL gives the award to a player or players each year for excellent play on the field and for making a positive impact in their community.

Brees (*right*) and LaDainian Tomlinson with their Walter Payton Man of the Year awards

He was better than before too. He proved it by throwing for 4,418 yards in 2006, the most in the NFL. Three years later, Brees led the Saints on a thrilling journey to the Super Bowl. They beat the Indianapolis Colts on February 7, 2010, to become champions.

Winning the Super Bowl made Brees a sports megastar, and the Saints paid him like it. His salary soared after 2010. By 2018, Brees had earned more than $221 million in his career. His earnings ranked third all-time in money earned by an NFL player.

In 2010, Brees brought the Saints their first Super Bowl win.

Brees hands the ball to running back Reggie Bush during the Super Bowl.

Brees wants to put his money to good use. He started the Brees Dream Foundation to help people in need and people struggling with cancer. He gives money and time to groups that help people in New Orleans, San Diego, and other places. Brees's foundation has given more than $33 million to help people around the world.

PASSING
CHAMP

Brees throws a pass in his record-breaking game in 2018.

On October 8, 2018, Brees took the ball and stepped back to throw. He faked a short pass. Then he launched a deep throw to the right side of the field.

Teammates swarm Brees after he breaks the NFL's all-time passing record.

Teammate Tre'Quan Smith was there, wide open. Smith sprinted down the field for a 62-yard touchdown.

The score gave the Saints a big lead in a game against Washington. It was also a huge moment in NFL history. With the pass, Brees broke the all-time record for passing yards in the NFL. He finished the 2018 season with 74,437 yards, almost 2,500 more than any other player in league history ever had.

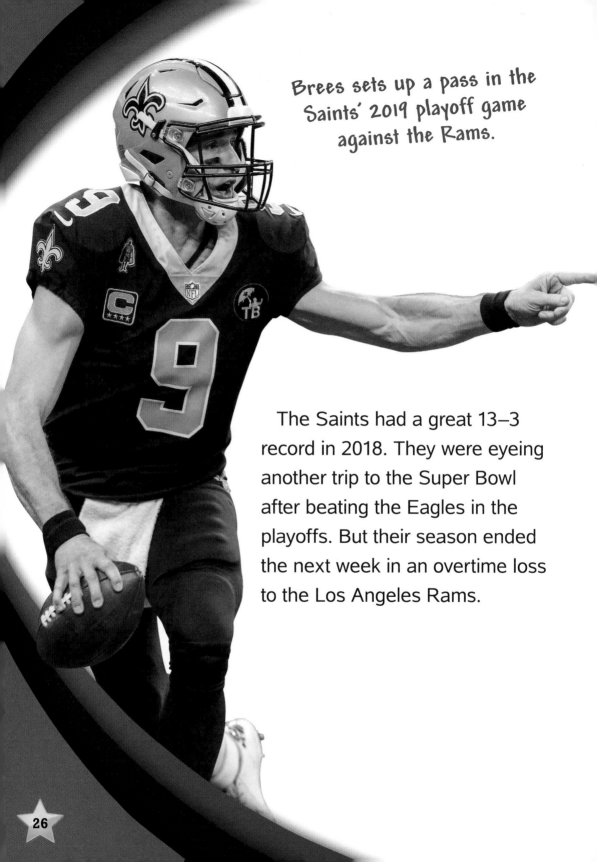

Brees sets up a pass in the Saints' 2019 playoff game against the Rams.

The Saints had a great 13–3 record in 2018. They were eyeing another trip to the Super Bowl after beating the Eagles in the playoffs. But their season ended the next week in an overtime loss to the Los Angeles Rams.

Brees turned 40 in 2019. He became one of the oldest players in the league. With his age and achievements, fans wondered if he was going to retire after the season.

But Brees wants another chance to win the Super Bowl. "I plan on being here next year and making another run at it," he said.

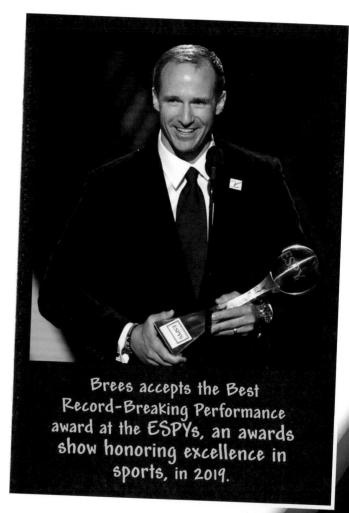

Brees accepts the Best Record-Breaking Performance award at the ESPYs, an awards show honoring excellence in sports, in 2019.

All-Star Stats

Some fans measure quarterbacks' greatness by how many games they've won or how many yards they've gained. Another good way to judge quarterbacks is by touchdown passes. After all, a quarterback's goal is to throw a touchdown pass each time he takes the field. Look at where Brees ranked after the 2018 NFL season in career touchdown passes:

Career Touchdown Passes

Player	Career Touchdown Passes
Peyton Manning	539
Drew Brees	**520**
Tom Brady	517
Brett Favre	508
Dan Marino	420
Philip Rivers	374
Ben Roethlisberger	363
Eli Manning	360
Fran Tarkenton	342
Aaron Rodgers	338

Source Notes

7 "Saints Rally Past Eagles 20–14, Will Host NFC Title Game," *ESPN*, January 13, 2019, http://www.espn.com /nfl/recap?gameId=401038958.

12 John Clayton, "Brees Agrees to Six-Year Deal with Saints," *ESPN*, March 15, 2006, http://www.espn.com/nfl /news/story?id=2368304.

17 Scooby Axson, "Dr. James Andrews on Drew Brees: 'Most Remarkable Comeback That I've Ever Treated,'" *Sports Illustrated*, June 13, 2014, https://www.si.com/si -wire/2014/06/13/james-andrews-drew-brees-remarkable -comeback.

20 Simon Evans, "Brees Proud of Saints Journey from Katrina," Reuters, January 20, 2010, https://www.reuters .com/article/us-nfl-saints/brees-proud-of-saints-journey -from-katrina-idUSTRE60K0BG20100121?feedType=RSS &feedName=domesticNews.

21 Julie Boudwin, "Drew Brees Tells Robin Roberts New Orleans 'Saved Me as a Person' after Katrina," *NOLA*, August 24, 2015, https://www.nola.com/saints/2015/08 /saints_qb_drew_brees_katrina_e.html.

27 Mike Triplett, "Drew Brees Plans to Return for 19th Season for 'Another Run at It,'" *ESPN*, January 21, 2019, http://www.espn.com/nfl/story/_/id/25813020/drew-brees -new-orleans-saints-sets-sights-making-another-run-it.

Glossary

agile: able to move easily and quickly

conference: a group of teams that play against one another

draft: an event in which teams take turns choosing new players

formation: an arrangement of players on the field for a certain play

interceptions: passes caught by the other team that result in a change of possession

poised: confident and calm

punt: kick the ball to the other team

rehab: a program to help someone heal from an injury

scholarship: money awarded to a student to help pay for school

scouts: people who judge the skills of athletes

snapped: put a football in play, usually by handing or throwing it to the quarterback

Further Information

Drew Brees Biography
https://www.ducksters.com/sports/drew_brees.php

Football: National Football League
http://www.ducksters.com/sports/national_football_league.php

Mack, Larry. *The New Orleans Saints Story*. Minneapolis: Bellwether Media, 2017.

Monson, James. *Behind the Scenes Football*. Minneapolis: Lerner Publications, 2020.

Saints Home
https://www.neworleanssaints.com

Savage, Jeff. *Football Super Stats*. Minneapolis: Lerner Publications, 2018.

Index

Photo Acknowledgments

Image credits: Wesley Hitt/Getty Images, p. 4; Chris Graythen/Getty Images, pp. 6, 14, 20; Todd Warshaw/Icon Sportswire/Getty Images, p. 8; Stephen Dunn/Getty Images, p. 9; MARLIN LEVISON/Star Tribune/Getty Images, p. 10; John Cordes/Icon Sportswire/Getty Images, p. 11; Owen C. Shaw/Getty Images, p. 12; Wild -Strawberries/Getty Images, p. 13; Brian Killian/NFLPhotoLibrary/Getty Images, p. 15; Tom Szczerbowski/Getty Images, p. 16; James R. Morton/NFLPhotoLibrary/ Getty Images, p. 17; Kevin C. Cox/Getty Images, p. 18; Dave Einsel/Getty Images, p. 19; Donald Miralle/Getty Images, p. 21; Al Diaz/Miami Herald/MCT/Getty Images, p. 22; Bob Snow/Macon Telegraph/MCT/Getty Images, p. 23; Sean Gardner/Getty Images, pp. 24, 25; Jordon Kelly/Icon Sportswire/Getty Images, p. 26; Kevin Winter/ Getty Images, p. 27.

Cover image: Patrick Smith/Getty Images.